The True Story of

THE FIRST THANKSGIVING

Colleen Adams

PowerKiDS press.

New York

Published in 2009 by The Rosen Publishing Group, Inc.
29 East 21st Street, New York, NY 10010

First Edition

Editor: Nicole Pristash
Book Design: Kate Laczynski
Photo Researcher: Jessica Gerweck

Photo Credits: Cover, pp. 1, 5, 11, 17, 21 © Superstock.com; pp. 7, 9 © Getty Images, Inc.; pp. 13, 15 © Northwind Pictures; p. 19 Shutterstock.com.

Library of Congress Cataloging-in-Publication Data

Adams, Colleen.
    The true story of the first Thanksgiving / Colleen Adams. — 1st ed.
        p. cm. — (What really happened?)
    Includes index.
    ISBN 978-1-4042-4476-4 (library binding)
    1. Thanksgiving Day—Juvenile literature. I. Title.
    GT4975.A28 2009
    394.2649—dc22

                                        2007052797

Manufactured in the United States of America

CONTENTS

WHAT IS THANKSGIVING?

Thanksgiving is a day Americans spend thinking about all the things they are thankful for. People who **celebrate** Thanksgiving spend time with their families and eat a big, special dinner with turkey and other tasty food. The **tradition** of Thanksgiving began with the Pilgrims, who settled in Plymouth, Massachusetts, in 1620. There are many **myths** about how the first Thanksgiving was celebrated, though.

Canada celebrates Thanksgiving as well. Canadian Thanksgiving takes place on the second Monday of October.

Do you want to know what really happened on the very first Thanksgiving? Let's look at what many people think happened and what the truth really is!

The Pilgrims and the Wampanoag Indians held the first Thanksgiving celebration in the fall of 1621. The exact date of the celebration, shown here, is unknown.

A NEW BEGINNING

The story of the first Thanksgiving begins with the Pilgrims. In the early 1600s, some people in England wanted to break away from the Church of England. They wanted to do this because they did not have the **freedom** to practice their own **religion**. They decided to leave England and travel to the **New World**.

The Pilgrims left England on a ship, called the *Mayflower*, on September 16, 1620. They hoped that starting a new life would give them the freedoms they did not have in England. Some of the Pilgrims also wanted to find **adventure** in a new land.

Here the Mayflower *is seen leaving Plymouth, England, in September 1620. The ship carried 102 men, women, and children to the New World.*

A LONG TRIP

The Pilgrims' trip lasted 66 days. Several storms tossed the *Mayflower* around on the ocean and made the trip very hard. The food and water supplies were almost gone by the time the ship reached land.

The Pilgrims landed in the New World in late December 1620. They named their settlement Plymouth. It is believed that the Pilgrims landed on Plymouth Rock. However, **historians** never found a description of where exactly the Pilgrims came ashore. The rock was not written about until years later. Because of this, the truth about whether the Pilgrims landed on Plymouth Rock may never be known.

Here the Pilgrims are seen coming ashore in North America, in December 1620. Many Pilgrims had become sick while on the Mayflower, so they were happy to leave it behind.

WINTER IN PLYMOUTH

The first winter in Plymouth was very hard. Those who were healthy had to take care of the sick, build houses, and plant crops. The Pilgrims were also worried about the Native Americans who already lived on the land. These Native Americans were part of the Wampanoag **tribe**. The Pilgrims were not sure if the Wampanoags would welcome them.

On March 16, 1621, an Algonquian Native American named Samoset came to Plymouth. He told the settlers who he was, and he talked peacefully with them. Soon after, Samoset brought Squanto, a member of the Wampanoag tribe, to help the settlers.

Samoset (center) walked right into the middle of Plymouth Colony without warning. This surprised the Pilgrims. It surprised them even more when Samoset spoke English!

SQUANTO HELPS THE PILGRIMS

Squanto became friends with the Pilgrims. He showed them the best places to fish and hunt. He taught them how to plant corn and use spices in their cooking. Soon, the settlers were feeling stronger. Colonist William Bradford wrote in his journal that the Pilgrims would not have lived without Squanto's help.

Samoset and Squanto set up a meeting between John Carver, the leader of the Plymouth settlement, and Massasoit, chief of the Wampanoag tribe. They signed a peace **treaty**. The Pilgrims did not have to worry about trouble with the Wampanoag tribe anymore.

The peace agreement made between the Wampanoags and the Pilgrims stated that they would not hurt or steal from one another. Each side promised to help the other.

The signing of the treaty, shown here, was important to both the Pilgrims and the Wampanoags. The treaty stated that each group would help keep the other safe from harm.

REASONS TO CELEBRATE

By the fall of 1621, the Pilgrims had grown a lot of corn and other crops with Squanto's help. They had enough food to eat and some left over for the next winter. The Pilgrims decided to celebrate the **harvest** with a special gathering with the Native Americans. It was a day of food, games, and dancing.

Many believe that the Pilgrims called this celebration Thanksgiving. However, to the Pilgrims, a day of thanksgiving was spent in church. This harvest celebration was just a day to give thanks for all the food. The name Thanksgiving was not used until years later.

The Pilgrims brought vegetable seeds with them on the Mayflower to plant in their new land. They planted the seeds in gardens and fields, like the ones shown here.

THE HARVEST CELEBRATION

There are many myths about what happened when the Pilgrims and Native Americans gathered to celebrate. One myth is that the Pilgrims and Native Americans ate together at a big table one afternoon. It is now known, however, that the harvest celebration lasted for three days, not one. They did not sit down to eat, either. Instead, they stood up and likely ate with their fingers!

The Pilgrims and Native Americans did a lot more than eat that day. The men and boys took part in running and jumping games. There was even singing and dancing.

This painting shows the Wampanoags and the Pilgrims celebrating what is known as the first Thanksgiving. Around 50 Pilgrims and 90 Native Americans celebrated together for three peaceful days.

NO TURKEY?

When people gather now for Thanksgiving dinner, they eat foods such as cranberry sauce, **potatoes**, and pumpkin pie. Many believe that the Pilgrims ate these foods, too. However, the Pilgrims and Native Americans did not have those foods. Instead, they ate boiled pumpkin, fruit, nuts, squash, and beans.

The Pilgrims had a lot of foods to pick from at the first Thanksgiving. They likely ate deer meat, duck, and some seafood, such as fish and clams.

Eating turkey at Thanksgiving dinner has become a Thanksgiving **custom**. Many historians think, though, that the Pilgrims and Native Americans may not have eaten turkey at the celebration. The Pilgrims and Native Americans had turkeys around, but no one knows for sure whether they ate them that day.

This picture shows foods that people eat on Thanksgiving today. However, the Pilgrims and Indians may not have eaten some of these foods, such as turkey, celery, and potatoes.

HOW THANKSGIVING BECAME A HOLIDAY

Another myth that people believe is that the Pilgrims celebrated the harvest every year after the first harvest. It has been proven, however, that the Pilgrims celebrated the harvest only when they had plentiful crops. Thanksgiving did not happen every year until much later. This is one of the biggest myths of Thanksgiving.

In 1863, President Abraham Lincoln made Thanksgiving the last Thursday of November. This was the first time it was stated that a day of thanksgiving was to be celebrated every year. This is when the United States still celebrates Thanksgiving today.

This family has gathered together for a meal on Thanksgiving Day. Some things have changed since the first celebration, but the idea of giving thanks has not.

WHAT REALLY HAPPENED?

The Pilgrims' idea of giving thanks for their harvest has become a tradition that has lasted hundreds of years. Many stories about what happened on that day of celebration have come about since. However, most of these stories have been proven wrong.

Did the Pilgrims land on Plymouth Rock? Did the Pilgrims and Native Americans gather together at one big table for dinner? Did they eat turkey? Many questions have been answered, but some may remain a mystery. Whatever the truth is, giving thanks and spending time with family every year is an important tradition. It will be enjoyed for many years to come.

GLOSSARY

adventure (ed-VEN-cher) An uncommon or fun thing to do.

celebrate (SEH-leh-brayt) To honor an important moment by doing special things.

custom (KUS-tum) A practice common to many people in an area.

freedom (FREE-dum) The state of being free.

harvest (HAR-vist) A season's gathered crop.

historians (hih-STOR-ee-unz) People who study the past.

myths (MITHS) Stories that people make up to explain things that happen.

New World (NOO WURLD) North America and South America.

potatoes (puh-TAY-tohz) White vegetables that grow in the ground.

religion (rih-LIH-jen) A belief in and a way of honoring a god or gods.

tradition (truh-DIH-shun) A way of doing something that has been passed down over time.

treaty (TREE-tee) An agreement, signed and agreed upon by each party.

tribe (TRYB) A group of people who share the same customs, language, and family members.

INDEX

WEB SITES

Due to the changing nature of Internet links, PowerKids Press has developed an online list of Web sites related to the subject of this book. This site is updated regularly. Please use this link to access the list:
www.powerkidslinks.com/wrh/thanks/